Magical Numbers

Ori Oasis
OrisOasis.com/OriKids

ISBN-10: 0615948944
ISBN-13: 978-0615948942

NOTE TO PARENTS

My spiritual path has always been a big part of my life. So it was only natural that when I became a mother, I would want to share that part of my life with our children as well. In my search, I have found plenty of beautiful children's books but found it impossible to find one that incorporates spirituality with the basic things a child must learn. I am not saying there aren't any out there but as of yet, they have not crossed my path. So I decided to create my own. Much to my surprise, my family and friends not only loved the idea, but encouraged me to share it with the world. Whether this is the first of its kind, I do not know. My only desire is that after this, more books like these will be readily available for those who seek them.

DEDICATION

To our Ancestral family who paved the way,
to our children who are willing to walk that path,
and to the family members seeking to aide them on their earthly journey,

Thank You.

.

ACKNOWLEDGMENTS

To loved ones near and far who are guiding me from the other side,
To the love of my life for always allowing room for my creativity to flourish and grow,
To our boys for always inspiring me to do more,
To my soul sister for helping me expand my dreams further than I could even imagine,
and to all, whether great or small, that have encouraged me in their own way,
Thank you a for being there for me.

Ori

Numbers are magical symbols. Let's see what they can do.

0

Zero

Zero is the number source.

The great cosmic egg.

By the power of 0,
I can create and do anything.

1

One

One is the number of will.

One is the force that gives you energy.

By the power of 1, my will shall be done.

2
Two

Two is the number of choice.

There is always a choice.

By the power of 2,
I always get to choose.

3

Three

Three is the number of spirituality.

From spirit comes creativity.

By the power of 3, I can create a happy life for me.

4
Four

Four is the number of stability.

From the four elements comes balance.

By the power of 4, I can open any door.

5

Five

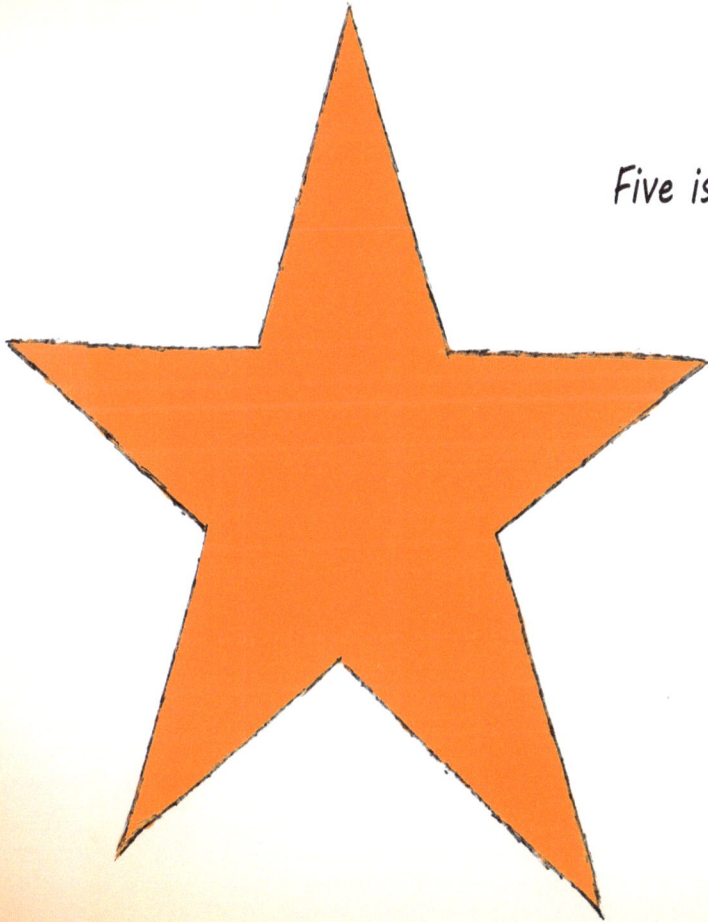

Five is the number of freedom.

When you feel free,
you can do anything.

By the power of 5,
my spirit will thrive.

6

Six

Six is the number of harmony.

From harmony comes peace.

By the power of 6,
I can create my own spiritual mix.

7
Seven

Seven is the number of return.

Your efforts always come back to you.

By the power of 7, I can make my life on earth heaven.

8

Eight

Eight is the number of cycles.

Everything happens in cycles.

By the power of 8, my desires flow freely
from my spiritual gates.

9

Nine

Nine is the number of new beginnings.

All things become new again.

By the power of 9, I can start a new life anytime.

1 8 2 6

9

4

Now I can use these symbols, too!

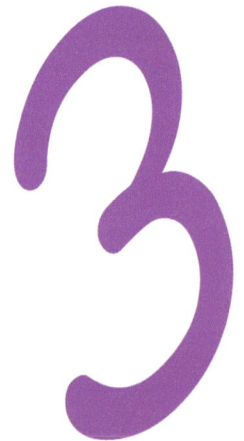

0 7 5 3

ABOUT THE AUTHOR

Nothing is ever happenstance and this life was brought to me because we asked for each other.

As well as being a wife and mother, I am the owner and creator of Ori Oasis and OrisOasis.com. For over twelve years, I have done Astrology readings, channeling, oracle readings, as well as being a mentor to others.